MIND BLOWING! THE BRAIN

MEMO

by Joyce Markovics

Cherry Lake Press
Ann Arbor, Michigan

Cherry Lake Press

Published in the United States of America by Cherry Lake Publishing Group
Ann Arbor, Michigan
www.cherrylakepublishing.com

Reading Adviser: Beth Walker Gambro, MS Ed., Reading Consultant, Yorkville, IL
Content Adviser: Heather A. Lau, MD MS, Pediatric Neurologist
Book Designer: Ed Morgan

Photo Credits: © freepik.com, cover and title page; © freepik.com, TOC; © HBRH/Shutterstock, 4; © Olga Popova/Shutterstock, 5 top; © Chursina Viktoriia/Shutterstock, 5 bottom; © freepik.com, 6; © freepik.com, 7; © EA Photography/Shutterstock, 8; © Andrey_Popov/Shutterstock, 9; © freepik.com, 10; © freepik.com, 11; © freepik.com, 12; © SciePro/Shutterstock, 13; © freepik.com, 14; © freepik.com, 15; © freepik.com, 16; © freepik.com, 17; © freepik.com, 18; © freepik.com, 19; Luigi Novi/Wikimedia Commons, 19 inset; © freepik.com, 20; © freepik.com, 21; © freepik.com, 22.

Cherry Lake Press is an imprint of Cherry Lake Publishing Group.

Library of Congress Cataloging-in-Publication Data

Names: Markovics, Joyce L., author.
Title: Memory / Joyce Markovics.
Description: Ann Arbor, Michigan : Cherry Lake Publishing, 2022. | Series: Mind blowing! the brain | Includes bibliographical references and index. | Audience: Grades 4-6
Identifiers: LCCN 2021035315 (print) | LCCN 2021035316 (ebook) | ISBN 9781534199552 (hardcover) | ISBN 9781668900697 (paperback) | ISBN 9781668906453 (ebook) | ISBN 9781668902134 (pdf)
Subjects: LCSH: Memory–Juvenile literature. | Memory–Physiological aspects–Juvenile literature.
Classification: LCC BF371 .M334 2022 (print) | LCC BF371 (ebook) | DDC 153.1/2–dc23
LC record available at https://lccn.loc.gov/2021035315
LC ebook record available at https://lccn.loc.gov/2021035316

Printed in the United States of America
Corporate Graphics

CONTENTS

FORGET-ME-NOT

A California woman named Jill Price can't forget. Since she was a child, Jill can remember exactly what happened almost every day of her life. "My memories are like scenes from home movies," says Jill. "Give me a date . . . and I can instantly tell you what day of the week it was, and what I did on that day."

Jill has hyperthymesia (hye-puhr-thy-MEE-zhuh). It's a rare memory **condition** that affects only about 60 people in the world! It gives them the ability to remember their life experiences in great detail.

President Theodore Roosevelt could memorize complete newspaper articles!

The average person can recall important events but often struggles to remember details.

Do you remember what you ate for dinner yesterday? Probably. But can you recall what you had for dinner on the same day last week or the month or year before? People like Jill can! So what exactly are memories? In simple terms, they're information that's stored in your brain.

The brain is an incredible pinkish-gray 3-pound (1.4-kilogram) **organ**. It stores all kinds of information, from pictures and smells to words and faces. When you experience or learn something, your brain figures out what information should be saved. But how exactly do we remember?

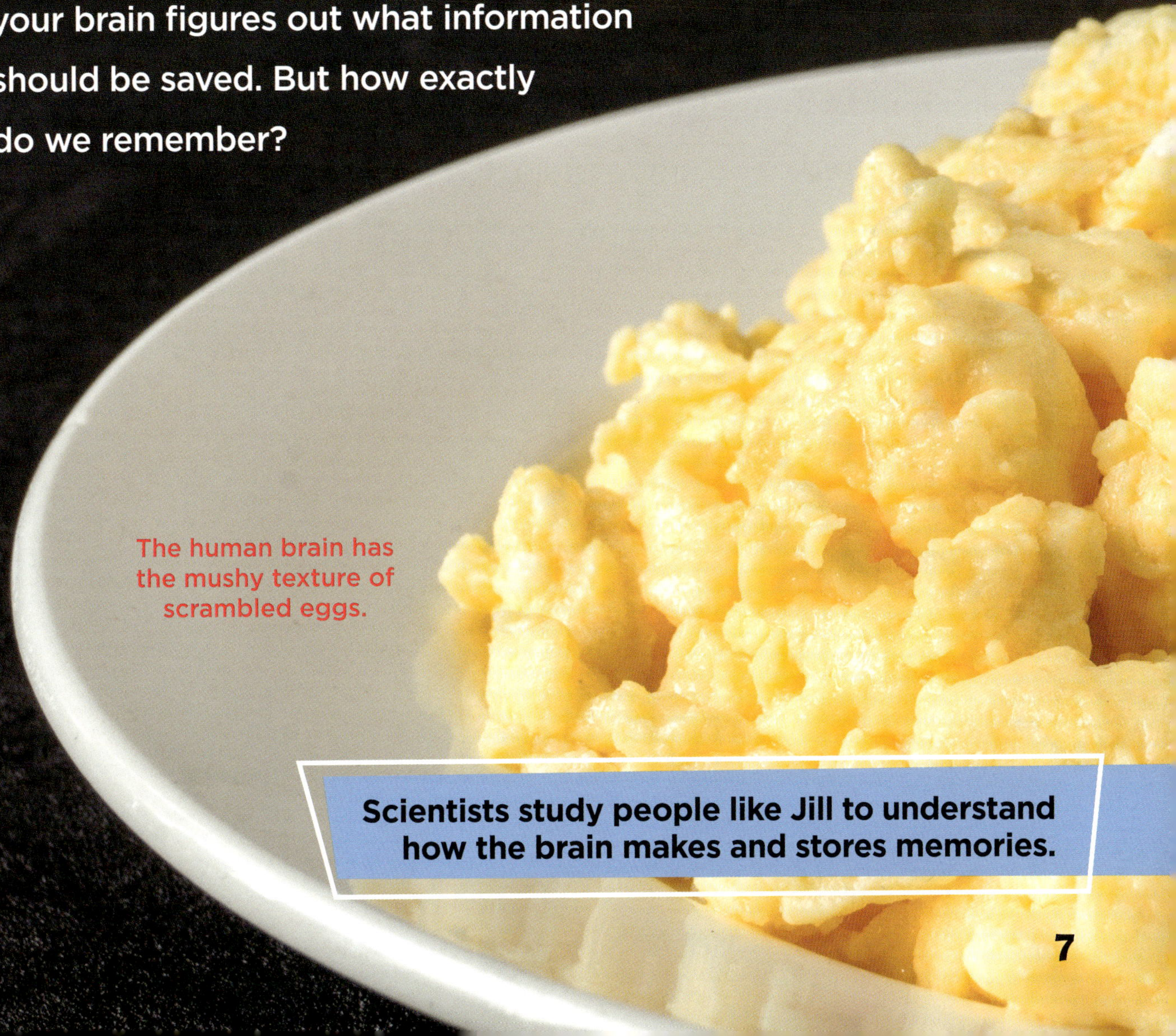

The human brain has the mushy texture of scrambled eggs.

Scientists study people like Jill to understand how the brain makes and stores memories.

IN THE BRAIN

Your brain has a lot of different parts. These parts work together to make it possible for you to remember. One of the main areas for memory is the hippocampus (hih-puh-KAM-puhs). Located deep in the brain, the hippocampus has two halves. It helps you form and store new memories.

The two halves of the hippocampus are shaped like seahorses.

Scientists figured out just how important the hippocampus is in 1953. At that time, surgeons removed **patient** Henry Molaison's hippocampus to treat his **epilepsy**. The surgery cured his epilepsy. But Henry could only form memories that lasted a few minutes. He completely lost the ability to store any new information.

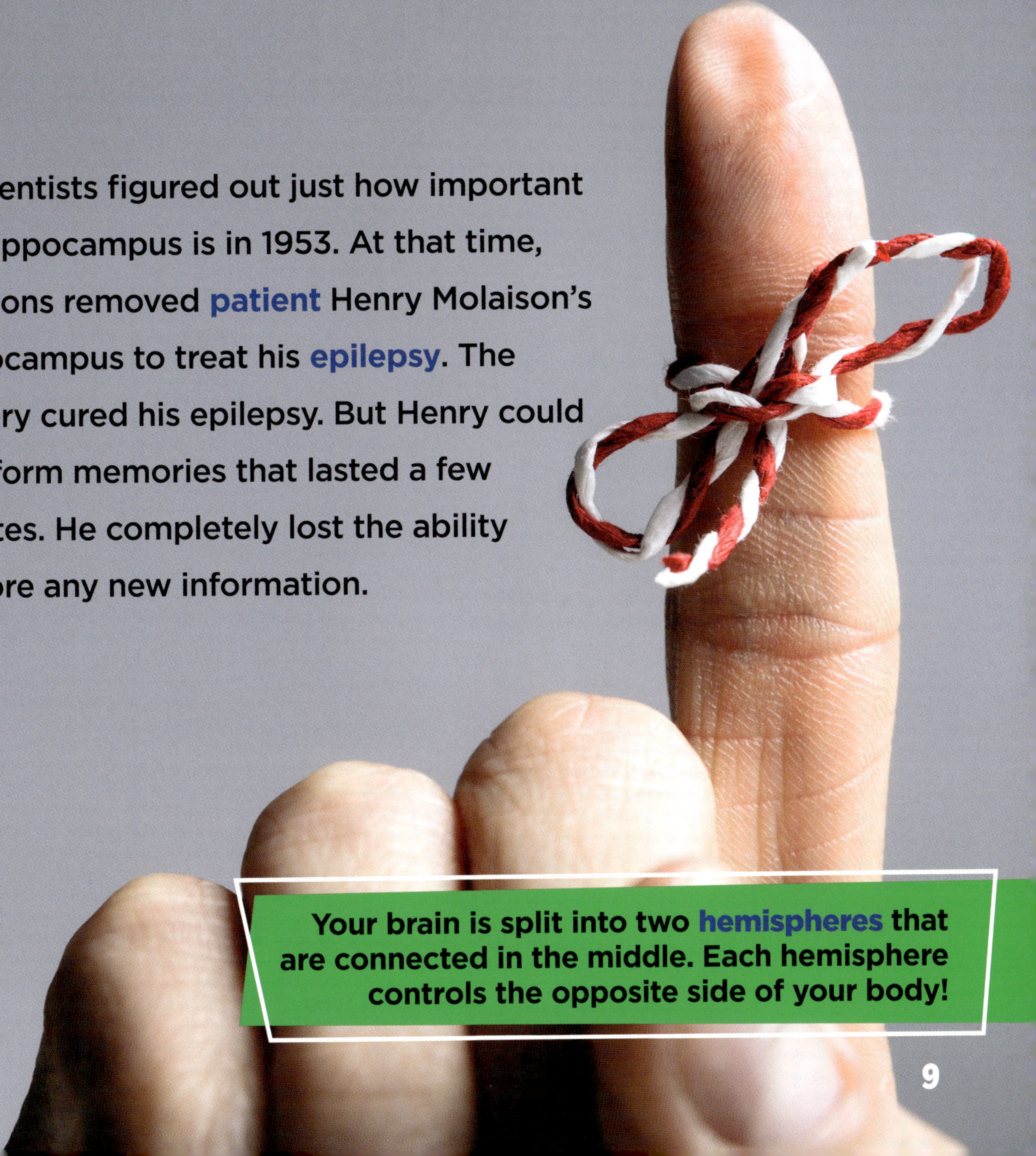

Your brain is split into two hemispheres that are connected in the middle. Each hemisphere controls the opposite side of your body!

Your cortex is working every time you do something, whether it's crunching on cereal or dancing to loud music.

In addition to the hippocampus, scientists think memories are stored in the cortex. The cortex is made up of gray, folded **tissue** that covers your brain like a wrinkly sheet. If you flattened it out, your cortex would cover a small bed!

Over time, information from memories stored in the hippocampus transfers to the cortex. Then the information becomes general knowledge, such as knowing that ice is cold or that rabbits hop. Scientists think this process mostly happens when we sleep.

Another part of the brain—the amygdala (uh-MIG-duh-luh)—links emotions and memories. This helps explain why strong emotional memories are hard to forget. Think about a time when you were really sad or afraid. That's your amygdala at work!

Each part of your brain is made up of billions of cells called neurons (NOO-ronz). Neurons carry messages throughout your brain and body using chemicals called **neurotransmitters**. Scientists think memories are somehow created through connections between neurons.

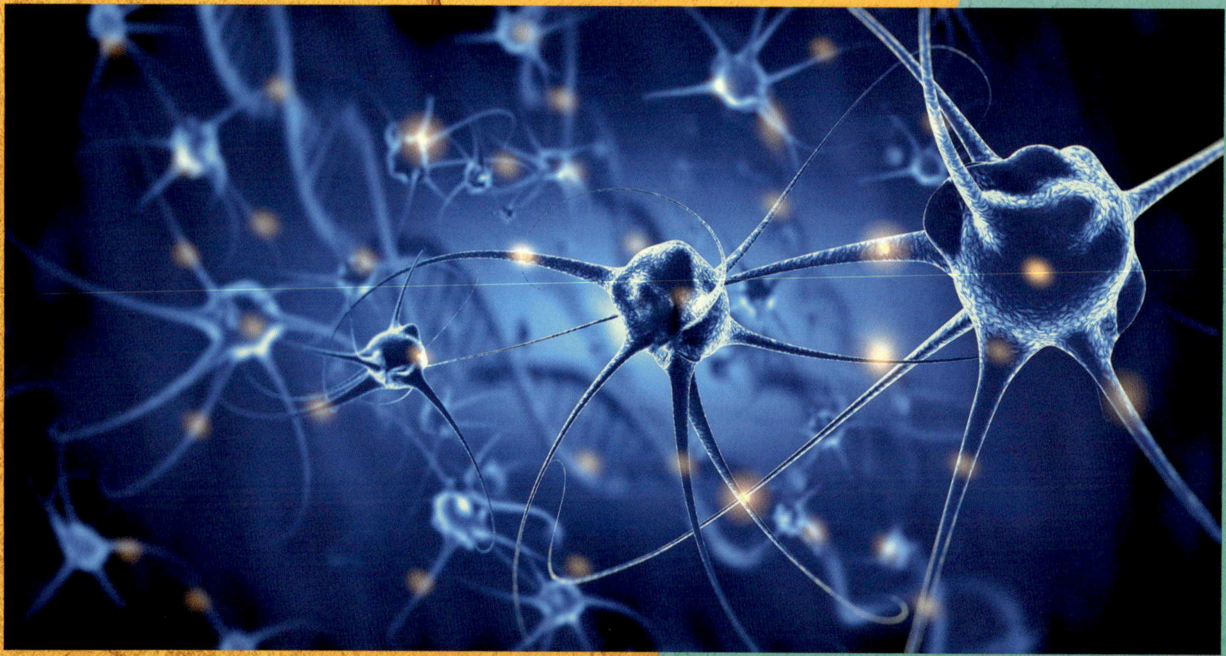

A neuron has a long tail, or axon, and branching threads called dendrites. A synapse is 20 to 40 nanometers wide. For comparison, the thickness of one sheet of paper is 100,000 nanometers!

Synapses link neurons together and make it possible for your brain to function. Without synapses, you wouldn't be able to learn and remember things. For example, when you sing a song or pet a dog, your synapses strengthen. So every time you pet a dog, your brain remembers it. Your brain can even anticipate how soft the dog's fur is before you pet it!

A bundle of neurons is a nerve. The brain is connected to nerves (shown in yellow) and the spinal cord (shown in white). The spinal cord is a big clump of nerves running down your backbone.

Your brain creates trillions of synapses until you're about ten years old. Then it starts pruning the ones you don't use.

MANY MEMORIES

Not all memories are the same. Scientists sort them into three main groups. A sensory memory connects to your senses, such as smell. For instance, when you sniff a flower in a garden, you might be flooded with memories of your grandma and her perfume. As it turns out, smell is closely connected with the part of your brain that deals with memory.

Short-term, or working, memories last seconds to hours. Remembering your outfit from yesterday is an example of a short-term memory. You are also using your short-term memory to understand the sentences on this page!

Long-term memories can last for years—or a lifetime. These include remembering your name, where you live, and how to brush your teeth. You can also probably recall important events, such your most recent birthday or a graduation.

When movements are repeated over time, a "muscle memory" is created for that task. We brush our teeth so often that we don't even have to think about it!

Memories are stronger when they're attached to emotions. That's why it's hard to forget a big celebration like a wedding or losing a loved one. Bad experiences, like breaking an arm, also help **forge** stronger memories. When we're under stress, though, it can be hard to remember even the simplest things.

Everyone can improve their memory! Neuroplasticity (noor-oh-pla-STIS-ih-tee) is the ability to make new connections in the brain. Scientists used to think only children's brains could change. In fact, with enough repetition, adult's brains can change too!

NO RECALL

Whether it's the result of a brain injury, disease, or disorder, some people have trouble remembering. A person with face blindness can't recognize familiar faces! Imagine not being able to remember your best friend's, aunt's, or even your own face! Many people with face blindness also struggle to remember landmarks or buildings.

Neurologist Oliver Sacks treated people with face blindness—and also suffered from it. In addition to not being able to identify people he knew well, like his own brother, whenever he tried to find a new way home, "I would be instantly and hopelessly lost," said Oliver.

Oliver Sacks wrote many books about unusual brain disorders. In 1985, he described a patient who was unable to recognize his own wife!

People with face blindness often have a **genetic** problem. This affects a part of the brain called the fusiform gyrus (FYOO-zuh-fawrm JYE-ruhs), which helps people recognize faces.

Other people lose their memories entirely. This can be caused by dementia (dih-MEN-shuh), a term that describes many different brain disorders. One form of dementia is Alzheimer's (ALTS-hye-muhrz). This disease often affects older people and worsens over time. The main **symptom** is memory loss.

More than 44 million people worldwide are living with Alzheimer's. Some people can live with the disease for more than 20 years.

Memory loss occurs when neurons in the hippocampus die. As the disease worsens, Alzheimer's patients forget their loved ones and even how to talk and walk. Experts are researching new ways to keep our amazing brains healthy. After all, according to Oliver Sacks, the brain is the "most incredible thing in the universe."

BRAIN GAMES

How good is your memory? With a friend, look at the photo on this page. Study it for 30 seconds. Then give your friend the book. Make sure you can't see the photo. Have your friend ask you questions about the photo, such as:

- What color shirt and hat is the person wearing?
- Does the person have short or long hair? What color is it?
- What is the person's eye color?

How did you do?

GLOSSARY

anticipate (an-TIH-suh-payt) to realize beforehand

condition (kuhn-DIH-shuhn) general health; fitness

epilepsy (EH-puh-lep-see) a medical condition of the brain that causes sudden, irregular movements called seizures

forge (FORJ) to create

genetic (juh-NET-ik) having to do with the way a person's characteristics are passed from one generation to another through genes

hemispheres (HEH-muhs-fihrz) the two halves of a round object such as a brain

neurologist (nuh-RAH-luh-jist) a doctor who specializes in the study of the brain and the nervous system

neurotransmitters (nuhr-oh-trans-MIH-tuhrz) chemical signals used by the brain to pass messages between neurons

organ (OR-guhn) a body part that does a particular job

patient (PAY-shuhnt) a person receiving medical care from a doctor

pruning (PROO-ning) removing extra or unnecessary material

synapses (SIH-nap-suhs) gaps between neurons where nerve impulses, or signals, travel

symptom (SIM-tuhm) a sign of a disease or other physical problem felt by a person

tissue (TIH-shoo) a group of similar cells that form a part of the body

FIND OUT MORE

Books

Mason, Paul. *Your Mind-Bending Brain and Networking Nervous System*. New York, NY: Crabtree Publishing, 2016.

Silver, Donald M., and Patricia J. Wynne. *My First Book About the Brain*. Mineola, NY: Dover Publications, 2013.

Simon, Seymour. *Brain: Our Nervous System*. New York, NY: HarperCollins, 2006.

Websites

American Museum of Natural History: Brain Introduction
https://www.amnh.org/exhibitions/brain-the-inside-story/brain-introduction

The Franklin Institute: Your Brain
https://www.fi.edu/your-brain/interactives

KidsHealth: Memory Matters
https://kidshealth.org/en/kids/memory.html

INDEX

ABOUT THE AUTHOR

Joyce Markovics has written hundreds of books for kids. She's fascinated by the human brain and all its complexities. She would like to dedicate this book to Joseph Lane, who lives on in the memories of his children, Ryan and Ashley, and his many loved ones.